The Riddle of the Sphinx

of the

Puzzles from Ancient Egypt

The Riddle of the Sphinx

of the

Sphinx

Puzzles from Ancient Egypt

TIM DEDOPULOS

CARLTON
BOOKS

The publishers would like to thank the following sources for their kind permission to reproduce the pictures in this book:

Alamy: /Robert Harding Productions: 12

iStockphoto.com: 2, 5, 8, 13, 14, 16, 40, 42, 45, 51, 65, 66, 74, 79, 82, 102, 104, 118

Thinkstock: 6, 11, 17, 22, 26, 29, 31, 33, 35, 39, 43, 44, 46, 57, 58, 59, 62, 68, 71, 78, 80, 84, 86, 89, 90, 94, 96, 99, 108, 110, 131, 137

THIS IS A CARLTON BOOK

by Carlton Books Limited
20 Mortimer Street
London W1T 3JW

Copyright © 2016 Carlton Books Limited

ISBN 978-1-78097-874-1

Project editor: Chris Mitchell
Text and puzzles: Tim Dedopulos
Design: Stephen Cary
Production: Alastair Gourlay

10 9 8 7 6 5 4 3 2 1

Printed in Dubai

CONTENTS

AUTHOR'S NOTE

In compiling this book, I have taken some horrible liberties with Ancient Egyptian culture, and with history in general. Sorry. Where puzzles clashed with reality, puzzles had to win. I have done my best to stay true to mythology, locations, units, and other factors as much as possible. As the mythic aspects of Ancient Egypt did not generally cause problems with puzzle design, I believe most of it to be at least broadly accurate. I hope so, anyway. Other aspects, however, did not do as well. In particular, any links I have made between puzzles and specific places are purely imaginary. So please take the historical content with a pinch of salt; I hope you enjoy the puzzles.

Tim Dedopulos, *May 2012.*

INTRODUCTION

O Mighty Sphinx, who will be remembered even when the world is old, and man dreams strange and impossible dreams. Ever your humble servant, I have obeyed your command and prepared for your edification and amusement a scroll of all manner of puzzles and riddles. None, of course, are as fine as your own riddle, but some I hope shall bring you some small satisfaction.

Some embody certain curious circumstances that I have come to learn of. A few matters are of direct practical concern while others are entirely abstract, belonging purely to the realms of Seshat, and if there is any enlightenment within it surely comes from She Who Scribes, and not from my own unworthy quill.

I have endeavoured to make the terms of each problem as clear as I am able. If there is any uncertainty involved, it comes from my own lamentable failings. I pray that all is to your satisfaction, Great Sphinx.

PUZZLES

"IF YOU SEARCH FOR THE
LAWS OF HARMONY, YOU WILL
FIND KNOWLEDGE"

Ancient Egyptian Proverb

CRATES 1

In the city of Sardes, the dockside storage area is arranged in a curious manner that makes theft easier to spot.

Crates of goods are stored in a grid seven piles long and seven piles wide. No pile is ever left empty, nor is any loaded more than seven crates high. In each row and in each column there is exactly one pile of each height, no more, no less.

Some piles are required to be higher than a neighbouring pile. These are indicated by an arrow which points to the lower pile.

From the sketch I have drawn here, can you calculate the number of crates on each pile of the grid?

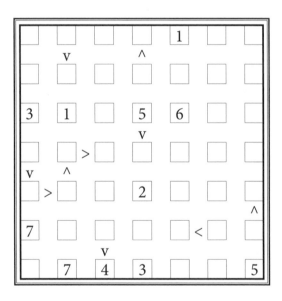

Solution on page 106

THREE LOAVES

Three loaves of bread are to be divided between five labourers. Each man must get pieces of identical size to his fellow workers, and no man may receive more than one piece of the same size. How would you divide the bread?

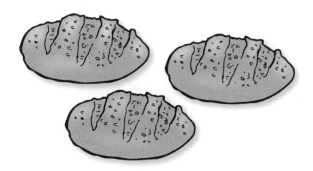

Solution on page 106

THREE BY THREE

H ave you ever wondered what makes a good game? I suggest that a good game must have both an element of strategy and an element of chance. A better player should be able to beat a lesser, but this should not be absolute. So consider the well-known child's game which uses a grid of three squares by three. Two players take turns to make their mark on an empty square, and win by filling a clear line of three squares before their opponent. Do I consider this a good game?

Solution on page 106

SHADOWS

I beg you, Strong Bull, turn your mind to this trifling issue. at a certain time of day, a pole that is 1 metre tall casts a shadow of 75 centimetres. At the same time, there is a tree whose shadow is 8 metres long. How tall is it?

Solution on page 107

RIDDLE OF THE SPHINX 1

Mighty Sphinx, you are of course known throughout the lands for your troublesome riddles, and no riddle is more famed than this:

WHICH CREATURE IN THE MORNING GOES ON FOUR LEGS, AT NOON ON TWO AND IN THE EVENING ON THREE?

Solution on page 107

UP AND DOWN

I have an interesting little diversion that is supposed to have originated in Mycenae. In the grid below is a selection of paired tiles. Each pair must be connected by an unbroken path of tiles that can travel both horizontally and vertically. No two paths can cross. No path forms a loop, not even a closed knot of a square of four touching cells. One square, indicated by a star, does not form part of the pattern; all the rest are taken up by the paths of tiles. Can you uncover them?

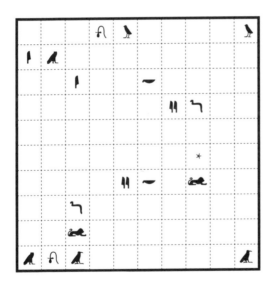

Solution on page 107

CONNECTIONS

L ord of All, in this problem, three pairs of numbers are connected through a mathematical operation to a common answer. What is the missing number?

Solution on page 108

CHARIOTS OF FIRE

A Royal chariot archer can fire eight arrows per minute and hit his target two-fifths of the time.

A Nile bowman can fire six arrows per minute and find his mark a third of the time.

On the battlefield a group of 15 chariot archers and a group of 25 bowmen prepare to fire. Which group will hit the most targets in the next minute?

Solution on page 108

DARK SQUARES 1

These boards are to be combined into one summary board, but they do so in a curious fashion. If a dark square is present on an odd number of boards, it is present in the summary, but if it is coloured on an even number of boards, it is not shown. What does the summary board look like?

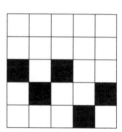

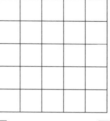

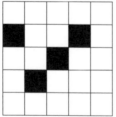

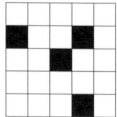

Solution on page 108

HIEROGLYPHS 1

In the equations scribed below, various whole numbers have been replaced with glyphs. Assuming that for each equation the calculations are performed strictly in the order they appear, what are the numbers?

$$\text{(glyph)} + \text{(glyph)} - \text{(glyph)} = 1$$

$$\text{(glyph)} \times \text{(glyph)} + \text{(glyph)} = 10$$

$$\text{(glyph)} - \text{(glyph)} + \text{(glyph)} = 5$$

$$\text{(glyph)} \times \text{(glyph)} \times \text{(glyph)} = 24$$

Solution on page 109

TILES 1

The right-hand tile relates to the left-hand tile in a consistent manner. What does the missing tile look like?

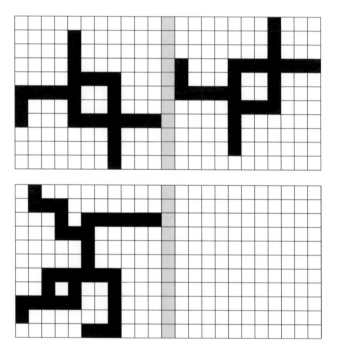

Solution on page 109

FULL BEAM 1

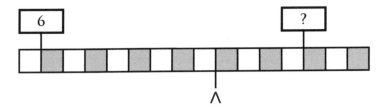

This beam is in balance over the pivot that is shown. You may assume that the beam and connecting rods are all perfectly stiff and counter-weigh each other perfectly, and that the marked divisions are of identical length. What is the weight of the block bearing the question mark?

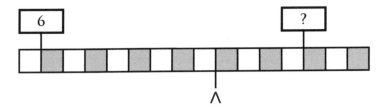

Solution on page 109

DOG AND HARE

A dog spots a hare 50 cubits distant, and gives chase. The dog will catch the hare after 125 cubits, but when the distance between the two is just 30 cubits, how much further will the chase have to run?

Solution on page 110

SACRED GRIDS

Consider these numbered grids. Each follows on from the one before. Where will the glyphs be in the fourth?

1

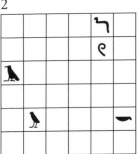

3

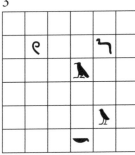

2

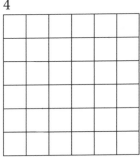

4

Solution on page 110

TACTICS

Mastery of tactics depends in part on awareness of opportunity. Consider the field displayed here. Take each square to be a *khet* in length. Each number represents an archer stationed in the field. There are obstructions in the field, which are not shown. They are considered to occupy a single square each. Each archer is to be thought of as reporting the number of squares in the field that he can see, vertically or horizontally, including the square he is on. So a man reporting four squares is able to see his own space and just three others. Archers do not obstruct each other, and do not stand on obstructions. No two obstructions are in horizontal or vertical contact. Can you calculate the precise extent of each man's range?

						5		13	
	5				14				
7									
	12						5		
				12		12			4
	11		2				9		
		5					12	17	
8			8		13				
		10						11	
									7
				10			15		
	11		8						

Solution on page 111

SQUARE OF NUMBERS 1

This square of numbers is a thing of potent magic. Its Heka is such that every row and column adds up to the same total, as do the two major diagonals. The pairs of numbers fit into the horizontal empty spots on the grid. What is the complete square?

		7		
		25		
17	5	13	21	9
		1		
		19		

14	22		23	6
4	12		10	18
20	3		2	15
11	24		8	16

Solution on page 111

SESHAT'S LOGIC

You well know, mighty Pharaoh, that we divide our day into twenty-four hours. Perhaps Seshat has touched me with her wisdom, for I foresee that the day will come when every hour will be deemed to have the same length, and each will be split into sixty divisions, minutes, in the Sumerian way. If that is not enough to ponder, consider this. The time is 05:41. What time will it be when these four digits next describe the minute?

Solution on page 111

THE ETERNAL

In Aaru, the eternally living enjoy their reward for a blameless life. The reed-field islands are as numberless as they are lush and bountiful.

In this design, a dominion of islands is marked out. It is possible to get to any island from any other, as they are interlinked by either single or double pathways. The pathways are straight, horizontal and vertical, do not bend or cross each other, and terminate invariably at an island. Each island bears a tally of the total number of pathways touching it. Where do the paths fall?

Solution on page 112

ANCIENT TABLETS

In the three tablets below, the three four-digit numbers are operated upon to produce a three-digit answer, represented by the letters shown. The process of operation is identical in each case. What is the answer to grid III?

I						
1	4	3	2			
3	6	6	5	H	A	A
5	9	0	8			

II						
2	1	3	1			
4	5	5	4	B	I	B
6	9	7	7			

III						
1	0	1	7			
2	9	3	3			
4	7	6	5			

Solution on page 112

THE MERCHANT

A merchant is travelling from Thinis to Abydos. Travelling is cooler than sitting still in the daylight, so he does not want to arrive until dusk, but he is tired and thirsty, so he does not want to arrive after dusk. If he sets his speed at 300 khet an hour, he will be an hour early. If he travels at 200 khet an hour, he will be an hour late. What speed should he set?

Solution on page 113

LABYRINTH 1

There is an art to the construction of the perfect labyrinth. Clearly, there are some well-established guidelines that are worth following. At the same time, however, it is important to recognise that for true security a less familiar element needs to be incorporated.

This trial will provide you with the basis for a labyrinth layout that is grounded in mathematics. The cells of the grid below each hold a number from 1 to 14. In any given row or column, some numbers may be duplicated. Your challenge is to block out duplicates so that no number is repeated in any single line, horizontal or vertical. In addition to that, you need to ensure that no two blocked cells are in horizontal or vertical contact with each other. It is also necessary to make certain that you can get from any unblocked cell to all others, moving orthogonally, without having to cross a blocked cell.

1	14	14	5	10	10	2	8	12	7
13	4	13	3	3	7	1	5	4	14
2	13	4	10	6	9	12	12	8	4
7	3	14	11	11	8	6	2	9	6
6	12	5	8	12	8	10	5	13	1
12	11	1	10	5	10	8	6	3	12
9	7	5	11	13	9	12	6	5	6
13	11	8	13	9	11	7	14	4	9
8	10	6	2	5	5	8	8	1	12
11	8	1	6	1	3	14	4	11	13
1	12	7	3	3	3	4	8	2	8
12	5	4	4	14	1	8	7	12	9
8	9	4	2	2	14	3	3	14	11
5	5	2	9	7	14	14	10	11	11

Solution on page 113

A JAR OF ALE

The Keeper of Ale found himself with a problem earlier. I suspect that you would have been able to advise him properly, Great One. He found himself with just three jars. The largest, an eight-hinu jar, was full of ale. The two smaller jars, measuring five hinu and three hinu, were both empty. He needed to prepare two four-hinu measures of ale. What is the most effective way that he could do so without resorting to guesswork or finding some extra measuring devices?

Solution on page 114

SUN SPOTS 1

This pattern follows a certain mathematical logic. How many points does the question mark represent?

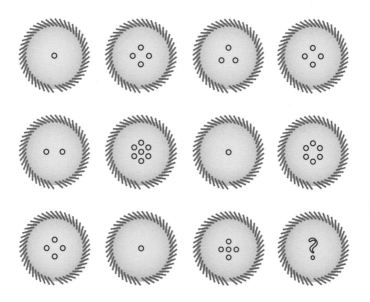

Solution on page 114

CHICKENS

A group of friends are at the local temple, buying a consignment of chickens. If each person pays 9 debens of copper, they will have 11 debens too much. If each pays 6 debens, they will have 16 too little. How many friends are in the group?

Solution on page 114

LABYRINTH 2

Can you find your way from the top of this labyrinth to the bottom?

Solution on page 115

LAST WILL

A wealthy merchant died recently, leaving his wife pregnant. In his will, it states that if the wife bears him a son, the boy is to get two thirds of the holdings, and the wife the remaining third. On the other hand, if she bears a daughter, the wife should get two thirds, and the daughter the remaining third. The gods, however, have been capricious. Three days ago, the wife gave birth to twins, one of either sex. What is your judgement as to the fair disposition of the man's goods according to his wishes?

Solution on page 116

THE RULE OF ORDER

The symbols in this labyrinth appear according to a strict order. If you uncover the underlying pattern, it will be easy to correctly complete the missing segment.

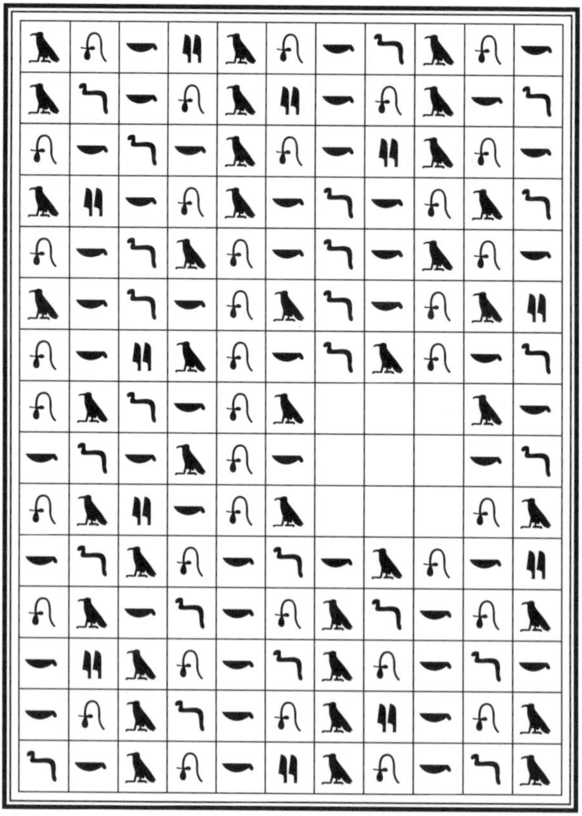

Solution on page 116

SEMERKHET'S TABLET

This curious tablet can be divided into four identical shapes. Each piece thus divided contains one of each of the five symbols, as shown. What is the division?

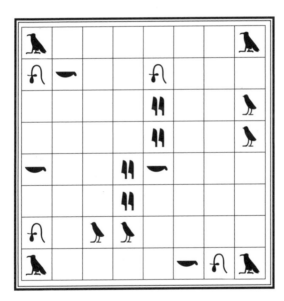

Solution on page 117

EQUAL SPACE

Certain members of the palace guard have drawn a problem to my attention. The division of living space – a relic of the past, undoubtedly – is proving somewhat unfair. Perhaps you would favour them by sorting out a more just division of accomodation?

I have taken the liberty of preparing a representation of the living space in question for you. For each guard, I have marked down the number of months that he has been in your service. I feel that it would be sensible to allocate each man a simple rectangular space equal in squares to the duration of his service to date. Can you enclose each man in a rectangular space exactly equal to his length of service, so that no two spaces overlap, and no space is left over?

	7					
	21					
				15		
		35				
				30		
			18			
	24					

Solution on page 117

POWER OF TEN

My Pharaoh, it may have occurred to you that we count in batches of ten. We have ten separate unique digits. When we write '10', we mean "One lot of ten, and none extra." '100' indicates one lot of ten times ten. But this is not the only way. The Babylonians, for example, count in batches of sixty, as did the Sumerians before them. It can be helpful to gain some practice with the idea of different counting systems. If one counted in batches of five, so that "100" meant twenty-five, what would the number ninety-five look like?

Solution on page 118

AHNEN AND BATA

A pair of labourers have been tending the trees in one of your ornamental gardens today, mighty Pharaoh. Ahnen and Bata were assigned one half of the garden each, the number of trees being the same in both halves. Ahnen started first, took the right-hand side of the garden, and began working. He had seen to three trees when Bata arrived, and declared that Ahnen was dealing with the wrong side. Ahnen obediently swapped to the left side. The men then worked through the morning. As noon approached, Bata finished his side of the garden, and then decided to help Ahnen get his half completed. Bata cared for six trees before the work was completed. Who tended the most trees, and by what quantity?

Solution on page 118

LABYRINTH 3

In this cunning labyrinth of numbers, you are required to move cautiously, horizontally or vertically, always stepping from 2 to 4 to 6, then 8, 0, and back to 2 again. Starting from a 2 on the top row, your task is to find a route to the bottom — and the sum of all of its steps, added together, must total 280.

2	4	2	4	8	2	6	2	4	2	0	2
2	6	8	6	4	2	0	8	6	4	6	4
6	2	4	8	2	4	6	4	8	8	4	0
6	4	2	0	6	2	2	6	4	4	8	2
8	2	4	2	8	8	4	2	2	2	0	8
0	2	6	4	6	6	8	6	8	0	2	6
2	6	0	6	4	0	2	8	6	6	4	4
4	6	8	0	2	4	0	8	4	2	6	8
2	6	6	8	6	6	8	0	2	0	2	0
4	4	2	6	8	6	6	0	6	6	4	2
6	2	4	2	4	4	4	2	0	8	6	0
8	8	6	4	0	8	6	6	2	4	6	2
0	4	2	8	2	8	2	4	0	2	4	8
4	6	8	6	4	2	4	8	8	6	8	6
6	2	0	6	2	0	2	2	4	2	0	4
2	0	2	4	6	2	8	0	2	4	6	0
8	4	4	6	8	0	6	4	6	0	8	2
2	8	6	8	0	2	4	0	2	8	0	8
6	0	6	0	6	4	8	8	6	4	2	6
4	2	4	6	2	6	4	0	4	2	8	4

Solution on page 119

GRAINS OF SAND 1

As the scribe would say — possibly talking about a small volume of sand — one amount plus its quarter is 16. What is the amount?

Solution on page 119

CHAINS

These numbers follow a strict sequence. what is the next term in the chain?

0

1

1

2

3

5

8

13

?

Solution on page 120

HIGH GRADE GRAIN

The matter of fairness in dealing is often critical. Yesterday, in the evening, our chief cook purchased wheat from one of the many merchants. He bought 12 hekats, of assorted qualities. Two hekats were of lesser-grade wheat, and were thus 40% cheaper than the regular grain. One hekat was low-grade, and 75% cheaper. On the other hand, two hekats were of high-grade grain, 25% more expensive than usual. The total cost was 219 deben of copper. How much is a single hekat of standard-grade wheat?

Solution on page 120

SIXES

There is a game that is played in the reaches of lower Egypt with small, polished cubes of bone or hard wood. The faces of each cube are numbered from 1 to 6, and they are cast to yield a number at random. Some wagering takes place on nothing so complex as the amount of sixes obtained. Do you think it is easier to roll six cubes and get at least one '6', to roll twelve cubes and get at least two '6's, or to roll eighteen cubes and get at least three '6's?

Solution on page 120

RABBITS

He Who Pacifies the Two Lands, it can be surprising how swiftly a situation can multiply to engulf all. For the sake of illustration, imagine that rabbits breed just once in every month, and give birth to just one rabbit of each sex. These young pairs mature over their first month, and then breed from the second month after their birth. How many rabbits will there be after twelve months, if all goes well for them?

Solution on page 120

MIGHTY MEHEN

It is well known that brave Mehen, the Coiled One, loops himself around Ra each night as the Sun journeys through the darkness of the underworld, helping to keep Apep the slitherer at bay. These voyages can be complex, far more so than the relatively simple course the Morning Boat steers through our skies during than the day. Priests of the Sun have scried the course of such a journey, but their minds lack the divinity required to untangle Mehen's precise movements. It is known that he forms himself into a single gigantic loop, tail caught by mouth, inside which Ra can benefit from his protective efforts.

In this representation they have prepared a square grid, the lines of which represent spaced which Mehen's body might occupy. Many cells of the grid contain a number which the priests have certified as representing the number of sides of that cell that Mehen's mighty body lies against. So a cell with the number 3 in has all but one side closed off by his length; a cell holding 0 is untouched, save perhaps at the very instant of a corner. For some cells, the priests remain sadly uncertain.

It would be most helpful to the poor priests if you would lend yourself to plotting the exact pattern formed by Mehen's body.

	2	1		2		2	3				
		2		1	3				2		2
2	2	0		2		1		2		1	2
		2	3	2			3	1		2	
	1		2	2		3	2		1	2	2
	2		3		2	2		3	2		3
		2	2	2		1		0		2	2
1		1	1			3		2			3
3			3	3	1		1	2	3		3
	1				2	3	1	2	1	1	2
	3										2
		1	3		3					2	

Solution on page 121

RECONNAISSANCE 1

Our scouts have gathered intelligence regarding a potentially hostile encampment on the borders of Punt. From outside the perimeter of the encampment, they have been able to ascertain the number of troop tents in any given slice of the groups. They have not been able to give absolutely precise locations, but they have confirmed that each tent is connected to an orthogonally adjacent tree. Every tree is occupied.

It would be of undoubted assistance to know the specific location of each tent. I am confident that your prowess will enable you to identify the precise positions with ease.

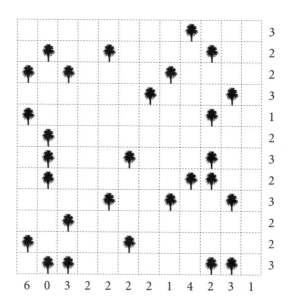

Solution on page 121

TOKEN GESTURE

This grid is made up of a number of pairs of tokens. Each individual token represents a number, and the totals at the end of each row and column are the value of the sum of each of the numbers in that line. What value does each token hold?

30

39

28

21 25 26 25

Solution on page 122

CHAMBERS 1

This grid represents a problem of chambers. I am happy to note that the situation is hypothetical, rather than literal, but solving it will undoubtedly prove useful when it comes to preparing for that blessed day when you resume your place amongst the Gods.

In the diagram, you can see a range of numbers placed into a simple grid. Each number is part of a chamber. The chamber contains exactly as many floor tiles as the number on those tiles. So a floor tile containing a '1' is a self-contained single-square chamber, whilst a tile containing a '4' is connected to three other tiles like itself. Most of the numbers are hidden, but the grid is completely used. All the tiles in one chamber are connected by touching, and no chamber directly touches another chamber of the same size at any point. Diagonal connections are not considered to be touching. Your goal is to calculate the extent of each chamber.

				1	6			1	4
6	6	1			1		6	4	
			4		9				
		9	5		5			3	1
			1	5	5		1	3	
1	6					1			
		1	6	1	3		1	5	7
		6	1	6		3	5	5	1
		6	6		4				
9							2		
	1		1		7	1		1	8

Solution on page 122

DAMNED SOULS

Three types of souls stood in a pack before Anubis, for the weighing of the heart. As you would expect, virtuous souls were confident in their rectitude and always told the truth, whilst damned souls, consumed by their own iniquity, could do naught but lie. Those whose fate remained uncertain were less predictable, and could speak either truth or falsehood as they saw fit. In this pack, there were 90 souls, divided into three groups. It is known that one group of 30 was made up entirely of one type of soul, another was split exactly into halves between two of the three types, and the final group comprised an even mix of all three types, ten of each. In no particular order, one of these groups of 30 declared themselves all virtuous. A second group bemoaned their damnation. The final group announced that all its members were unsure of what would come. How many souls were truly of uncertain fate?

Solution on page 123

NUMEROLOGY

For this problem, the number in the courtyard is obtained through performing mathematical operations on the numbers in the towers surrounding it. The same process is applied to each courtyard. What number should be in the final courtyard?

8	4	3	9
14		**13**	
7	9	4	5

7	2	6	1
12		**?**	
3	6	3	4

Solution on page 123

YIELD

If these tiles

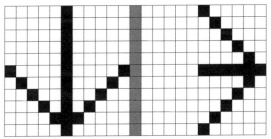

yield this result:

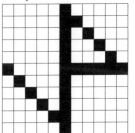

Then what do these tiles yield?

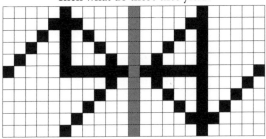

Solution on page 123

FULL BEAM 2

Pleaser of the Gods, consider this arrangement of beams, rods and weights. It is in exact balance. The beams and rods have been cunningly made so as to be perfectly stiff, and to counterweight each other exactly around the pivot, so that their weights may be discounted entirely. How much does the block with the question mark weigh?

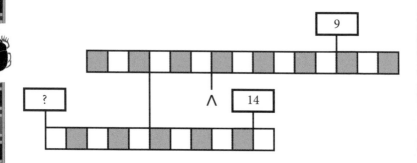

Solution on page 124

MYSTICAL WISDOM

This tablet contains long-forgotten mystic wisdom. It can be divided into four identical shapes, each containing the eight symbols shown below. What is the division?

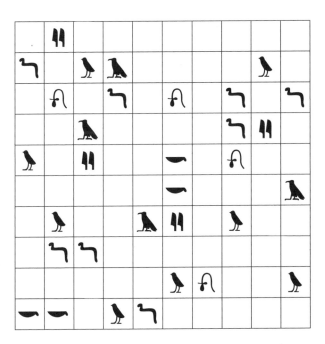

Solution on page 124

LINE OF FIRE

—⟫◆⟪—

Each number represents an archer stationed in the field. There are obstructions to his line of fire, which are not shown but occupy a single square each. Each archer reports the number of squares in the field that he can see, vertically or horizontally, including the square he is on. So a man reporting four squares is able to see his own space and just three others. Archers do not obstruct each other, and do not stand on obstructions. No two obstructions are in horizontal or vertical contact. Can you calculate the precise extent of each man's range?

				7				6		
11		9					9			
			4			5				
		13		13						
7	9		9							
						8				
			6							
							6		9	9
				6		2				
		7			2					
	9						8		7	
	13			7						

Solution on page 125

BEAST FOR SALE

In a nearby market yesterday, I happened to overhear three men discussing the possible purchase of an exotic beast, priced at 24 debens. None of the men had quite enough to buy the animal outright. The first one said, "If I borrow half of the money you two have between you, I'll have enough." The second one said, "Well, if I borrowed two thirds of what you two have, I'd have enough with two thirds a deben left over." The third one said, "If I borrowed three quarters of the money you two are carrying, I'd be able to buy it with one and a half debens remaining." How much does each man have?

Solution on page 125

SHARES

The just distribution of rewards can quickly become a matter of some complexity. Consider the matter of shares. There are 10 people who are to share 10 hekats of grain, but not evenly. The first person receives the largest share; each subsequent person gets 1/8th of a hekat less than the person immediately before. If there is to be no grain left over, then what is the largest share?

Solution on page 125

THE SNAIL

A snail accidentally falls into an earthy pit that is four and a half cubits deep. Trying to get out, it climbs up two cubits on its first day, but slips back down one cubit during the night. The process is tiring, and every subsequent day it climbs, it manages to go only 90% as far as the day before. It still slips the same distance during the night, however. When will it escape (or be forced to accept its new home)?

Solution on page 126

SEQUENCES 1

T hese grids form a sequence, a progression as unto the march of time itself. What should the fourth grid look like?

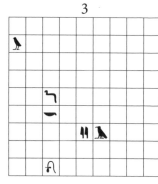

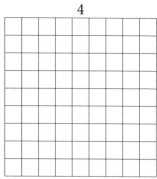

Solution on page 126

LABYRINTH 4

What is the route you need to take to get from the entrance of this labyrinth to its exit?

Solution on page 127

INHERITANCE

Three sons inherit 30 precious jars from their father, to be divided evenly. Ten of the jars are full of valuable unguents. Ten more are half-full. The remaining ten are empty. How can the jars be distributed so that each son gets his full share of ten containers and five full measures of unguent, and also receives at least one of each type of jar?

Solution on page 127

CRATES 2

I am informed that the Sardesian dock managers help to while away
the time by contriving increasingly tricky grids for the workers to pile
crates onto. To recap, each square of the grid holds a pile of between 1
and 7 crates. Each row and column holds exactly one of each size of pile,
and some piles are specified as being larger than others. Completing the
grid pattern from the arrangement shown here should offer you a certain
amount of diversion.

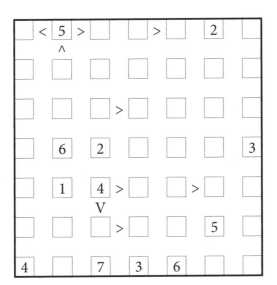

Solution on page 128

NAQABA

Consider these game boards, which I am told come from Naqaba.

If

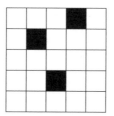

is worth 29 and

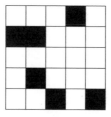

is worth 82, then how much is

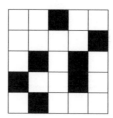

worth?

Solution on page 128

GRAINS OF SAND 2

Turn your mind, if you will, to a large heap of sand. If you take one grain away, it is still a heap. Keep taking grains away, one by one, and the heap will slowly shrink, but it remains undeniably still a heap. How about when there is just one grain left? Is it still a heap? If not, when did it stop being a heap? Something is clearly wrong, but what?

Solution on page 129

DATES

A quantity of dates, together with two-thirds of itself, has a third of its total number taken away to yield 10. What is the quantity?

Solution on page 129

SQUARE OF NUMBERS 2

>―◆―

This magical square of numbers is so cunningly devised that its every row and column add up to the same total, as do its two major diagonals. The sets of three numbers each fit into one of the empty horizontal groups on the grid. But where do they go?

			41			
			17			
			49			
13	31	7	25	43	19	37
			1			
			33			
			9			

18, 36, 12	21, 39, 8
46, 15, 40	22, 47, 16
2, 27, 45	42, 11, 29
30, 6, 24	26, 44, 20
38, 14, 32	34, 3, 28
10, 35, 4	5, 23, 48

Solution on page 129

TIME DIAL

A mechanical time-measuring device takes the form of a circle, with sweeping bars that move at different rate. The shortest bar makes a complete rotation two times a day, measuring 12 hours of light and 12 of darkness. The middle bar makes a complete rotation once each standard hour, as is considered to indicate sixty divisions of a minute. The longest bar, which moves fastest, makes a complete rotation sixty times an hour, once every minute. At exactly 8 o'clock, the short bar will be two-thirds of the way around the face, whilst the other two will be precisely vertical. To the nearest second, what will be the time when the three bars next align together?

Solution on page 130

PATH OF AARU

The heavenly reed fields are a beautiful paradise of peace and contentment. Those virtuous enough to dwell amongst them take their leisure amongst the islands. Naturally, in any dominion, it is possible to move from any one island to any other, though the route may not always be direct. The paths of Aaru are straight, never deviating nor crossing one another, although some are singular, and some are parallel double-paths. In this illustrated dominion, the islands alone are shown, and each island proudly displays the number of paths that touches it. How do the islands connect?

Solution on page 130

DIGITS

In the three tablets below, the three four-digit numbers are operated upon to produce a three-digit answer, represented by the letters shown. The process of operation is identical in each case. What is the answer to grid III?

I							
1	7	6	6				
2	1	4	5	E	B	F	
4	0	0	0				

II							
0	9	1	7				
1	8	1	6	C	G	D	
5	0	0	0				

III							
4	9	3	9				
2	7	4	1				
6	0	0	0				

Solution on page 131

BOUNCE

Consider this, mighty one. Bes, standing on a table, drops a ball from 1.44m above the floor. Each bounce, it regains precisely three quarters of the maximum height that it knew previously. It will stop when its maximum height is less than 1cm from the ground. How many bounces will this take?

Solution on page 131

RIDDLE OF THE SPHINX 2

> THERE ARE TWO
> SISTERS. ONE GIVES BIRTH
> TO THE OTHER AND SHE,
> IN TURN, GIVES BIRTH TO
> THE FIRST. WHO ARE THE
> TWO SISTERS?

Solution on page 131

MYCENEAN

This Mycenean grid is rather challenging, but it cannot be said that it is not entertaining or salutory. Paired tiles have to be connected by a single, unbroken line of tiles, connected horizontally or vertically without any redundant loops. No two lines cross. Two indicated tiles play no part, but the rest of the grid is filled. Can you find the paths?

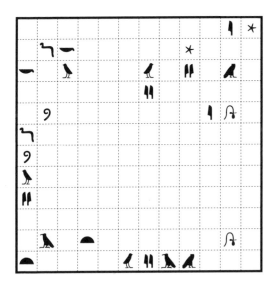

OASES

This problem links three pairs of numbers to a common answer, through varied mathematical operations. What is the central number?

Solution on page 132

DARK SQUARES 2

The dark squares on these four boards need to be combined into a summary board. They do not combine simply, however. If a square is dark on just one board, or on all four boards, then it is dark on the summary board. Otherwise, it remains unshaded. What does the summary board look like?

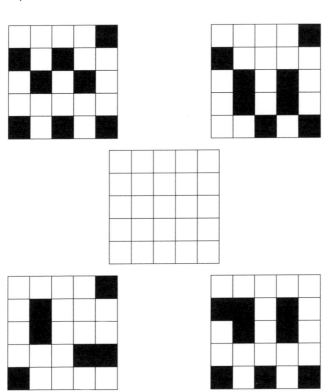

Solution on page 133

GLYPH

Mighty Ruler of Truth, the equations shown here are accurate, save that the whole numbers involved in the operations have been replaced. Calculations are performed strictly in the order they appear on each line, so what are the numbers?

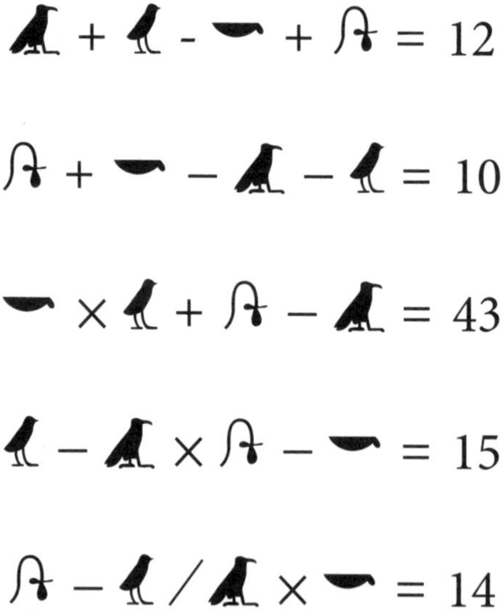

$$🦅 + 🦩 - 🪶 + 𓀭 = 12$$

$$𓀭 + 🪶 - 🦅 - 🦩 = 10$$

$$🪶 × 🦩 + 𓀭 - 🦅 = 43$$

$$🦩 - 🦅 × 𓀭 - 🪶 = 15$$

$$𓀭 - 🦩 / 🦅 × 🪶 = 14$$

Solution on page 133

ROOM SERVICE

The palace guardsmen that you generously accommodated recently have been greatly pleased with their new room allocations. They have been praising your wisdom far and wide. Accordingly, a second group, somewhat larger than the first, have also petitioned for similar treatment. It would be a generous gesture to so favour them. As before, I have made a note of the available space, and the number of months that each guard has been in service. I would appreciate it if you could take an instant or two to divide the space up so that each man is enclosed by a simple rectangular room, equal in squares to the length of his service. No rooms should overlap, nor should there be any space unallocated.

				8			
					18		
	10						
			12				
20							
		26				14	
			28				
				6			
				8			

Solution on page 134

BASE TEN

There are limitless ways, potentially, of organising how numbers are written. We write our numbers in base ten, where our numbers mean single units, batches of ten, batches of ten times ten, and so on. If the number 10240 is written in base 6, where 100 means 'thirty-six', how much does it represent in base ten?

Solution on page 134

OUTSIDE THE BOX

Imagine that three ornate but identical boxes are placed before you. Each holds two one-kite pieces. In one box, both kites are gold. In a second, they are both silver. In the third, there is one of each. You close your eyes, and pick one kite from one box, and then open them to discover that it is gold. What is the likelihood that the other kite in the box is also gold?

Solution on page 135

A WEIGHTY PROBLEM

The scales of justice are intimately familiar to all merchants, who are well versed in finding the correct weights and balances. There is benefit, of course, in carrying as small a selection of measuring weights as possible. What is the least number of measuring weights required to balance a load of up to 121 deben, and how much does each one weigh?

Solution on page 135

PRIESTS OF RA

The priests of Ra have returned with another set of divinations regarding the disposition of coiled Mehen during his nightly duties. They apologise that this is somewhat less certain than the last.

As before, Mehen's snaking body lies along some of the dotted lines in the grid below, forming one single gigantic loop. In each cell that they are certain of, the priests have recorded the number of sides of that cell which Mehen's body occupies. If you would extend your forbearance, they would be most grateful for your analysis of precisely where Mehen lies.

	2	3		3		3			3	3	
			2				0	2			
							3		2	3	
3	2				2	0				3	
		3			2		3		2	2	
3		3	1		2	2		2		2	
	1			3		0					
2	1			2		3					
	1			2			1		2	2	
			2	2	2		1		3		
2		1	1	0	2		2			1	
2			2			3			3		

Solution on page 135

UNLEASHED

A man is training his hound. He takes the beast a whole iteru from their home, and unleashes it. It proceeds to run home, and then immediately turns around and runs back towards the man. When it gets back to him, it immediately heads back for home again, and so on, running back and forth. At the same time, the man starts walking back towards home at a comfortable pace. The dog continues running until the man reaches the house. The creature is capable of running an iteru in one hour, and keeping that pace up for several hours at a stretch. The man on the other hand, walks just two-fifths of an iteru in one hour. How far will the hound run, from the moment of its release to the man's return to his house?

Solution on page 136

THE MAZE

In this maze of numbers, you are required to start somewhere on the top row, and finish by reaching the bottom row. You may move horizontally or vertically without restriction, totalling the value of the squares you step on as you go. However, stepping on or next to a zero wipes your score thus far. This is true even if you just pass diagonally adjacent to a 0, such is its power. Your task is to find a route totalling 170 points.

3	5	6	4	1	5		6	8	4	2	3
5	2	4	8	6	7			5	3	6	2
7	8	9	9	2	3	4		1	8	1	4
9	7	2	2	4	8	2		0	7	3	7
2	9	7	6	5	9				3	5	5
1	6	5	3	2	8				9	2	3
3	2	1	5	1	6	5			1	7	5
0	8	6	1	9	2	3			2	5	9
8	6	3	7	7	4	5		9	3	4	7
	2	7	8	3	3	7	3	5	6	1	8
			8	1	0	8	4	3	6	4	
6				6	5	3	7	2	5		
3	7	8			1	6	2	1			
3	4	8	4		9	0	4	3			
6	3	3			3	5	6	2			
2	3	5		2	4	8	6	7	3		
1	7	7		9	2	3	6	5	1		
6	0	3	5	7	6	4	1	8	9		
8	2	1	4	2	8	4	7	4	2	5	
9	3	5	7	3	8	2	1	2	7	4	3

Solution on page 136

RIVERS TO CROSS

The image shows a decorative divider.

Three priests are each escorting a novice priestess to a temple at Karnak. They meet whilst seeking to cross the Great River near Naqada. The coracle that is available to them to cross with can hold just two people, and it would dismay any of the young novices to be in the presence of an unfamiliar man without her guardian also being present. What is the most efficient way for the three pairs to cross, remembering that the boat cannot get back across the river on its own?

Solution on page 137

LABYRINTH 5

A twisting labyrinth is waiting to be unveiled in this test. In each horizontal or vertical line of this grid, you have to ensure that no number appears twice. Duplicates are to be blocked out. There are some restrictions, however. Squares are held to be in contact with each other either horizontally or vertically. No two blocked squares may be in contact, but every unblocked square has to remain in indirect contact with every other. When you have completed the pattern, there must be just one sprawling group of unblocked cells, with no number duplicated in any line.

6	7	1	8	5	5	7	8	11	11
9	4	7	10	3	8	1	14	10	5
1	3	4	2	2	14	9	8	9	4
3	3	8	4	4	7	10	2	5	14
12	12	7	4	8	9	9	4	7	8
11	5	6	1	5	2	14	9	13	8
2	1	2	1	13	12	12	6	4	4
12	13	2	6	2	7	5	7	14	13
10	9	12	2	14	5	2	9	4	13
5	7	13	5	7	10	12	3	13	2
5	8	9	9	12	2	11	6	2	6
8	9	5	10	9	11	5	4	11	7
2	6	9	6	7	12	4	13	12	11
13	8	3	7	13	9	8	3	1	7

Solution on page 138

FISHLESS

Two fathers and two sons are fishing in the Nile, they catch exactly three fish between them, but when they head home each of them has a fish. How can this be?

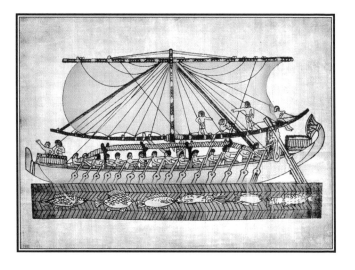

Solution on page 138

SUN SPOTS 2

This pattern follows a certain mathematical logic. how many points does the question mark represent?

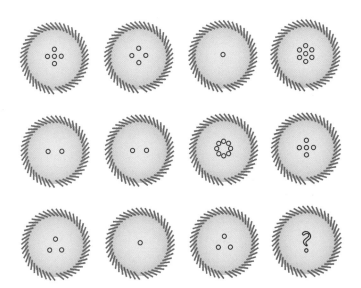

Solution on page 139

SIMPLE SYMBOLS

The appearance of symbols in this grid follows a strict order. The challenge here is to complete the missing segment by correctly identifying the pattern.

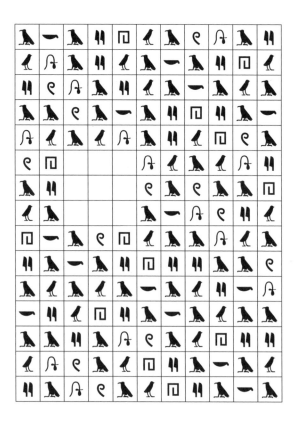

Solution on page 139

SEQUENCES 2

Consider this chain of numbers. They follow a specific sequence. What comes next?

2 4 6 30 32 34 ?

FIFTY LOAVES

A full cart of bread carries fifty loaves, but one particular slave is distributing less than that. If he gives nine men as many loaves as he can whilst making sure all have the same number of loaves, he has two left over. If he distributes the loaves likewise amongst four men, he is left with three. If his distributes them amongst seven men, there are five left. How many loaves are in the cart?

Solution on page 140

RECONNAISSANCE 2

Another tent camp has been causing your generals some small concern. As before, scouts have been able to examine the area from outside, and identify how many tents are to be found in each horizontal and vertical section. The trees are easier to locate precisely, but it is known that each tent is linked horizontally or vertically to one tree, although it may also abut others. Are you able to pinpoint the locations of each tent?

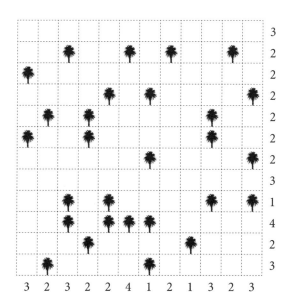

Solution on page 140

HIEROGLYPHS 2

There are several pairs of symbols in this grid. Each symbol has a numeric value. The numbers at the end of each row and column give the total found by adding all the individual numbers in that line. What value does each symbol have?

38

33

41

31   29   26   26

Solution on page 141

CHAMBERS 2

This is a slightly trickier problem of chambers. As before, the grid represents a space divided into chambers of assorted shapes and sizes. Each chamber contains one or more tiles of floor, connected from one to another either horizontally or vertically. The number on the tile tells you how many floor tiles that particular chamber encompasses. So, in an 8-tile chamber, each tile boasts the number '8'. However, most of the numbers have been obscured. Given that all the space is taken up, and that no chamber touches another of the same size horizontally or vertically, where are the chamber boundaries?

2	1						7		
					9		7		1
1			1	6	6		1	3	1
			6						3
3		1	7	7		1	6	1	4	4
9					7		1		
1					1				6
	1	2	1	3			1		8	1
	3	2							1	2
6				4		6		3		
1		1		1		1			3	

Solution on page 141

SHOTS ON TARGET

Your discerning ear for truth will surely unravel this issue swiftly, my Pharaoh. Three archers have been tested against each other, getting four shots at a target. Three points were awarded for a direct hit, two points for a near miss, and 1 point for a moderate miss. I am pleased to say that every archer managed at least a near miss. One managed four perfect shots, one managed two hits and two near misses, and one managed one hit and three near misses. However, they seem slightly confused as to the results. I have three statements from each archer, and for each of them, one of the statements is incorrect. Who scored what?

Ahmes:
> "I scored 9."
> "I scored 2 less than Baenre."
> "I scored 1 more than Djedhor."

Baenre:
> "I did not score the lowest."
> "The difference in scores between myself & Djedhor is 3."
> "Djedhor scored 12."

Djedhor:
> "I scored less than Ahmes."
> "Ahmes scored 10."
> "Baenre scored 3 more than Ahmes."

Solution on page 141

FIND THE NUMBER

The challenge in this puzzle is to find the number missing from the final courtyard. It is deduced by performing a set of calculations upon the four surrounding towers. Each courtyard works in the same manner. What is the number?

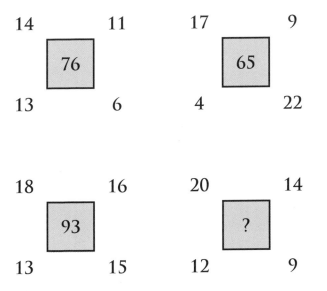

14		11		17		9
	76				65	
13		6		4		22

18		16		20		14
	93				?	
13		15		12		9

Solution on page 142

BOX OF GEMS

I magine for a moment that you are presented with your choice of two identical boxes. You select one, and you are then informed that both contain a gem, but one is worth twice as much as the other. You may switch your selection. Thinking about it logically, it is clear that you should swap, because if you go from low to high you get 100% as much again, but if you go from high to low, you only lose 50%. Your potential percentage gain is twice as much as your potential loss. You may then swap again, and everything that I said before remains true. How, then, are you ever to make a decision rather than to keep swapping the boxes?

Solution on page 142

TILES 2

If these tiles

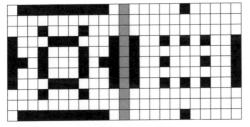

combine to form this one:

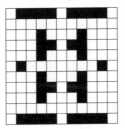

Then what do these tiles combine to form?

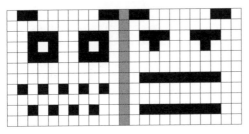

solution on page 142

97

FUll BEAM 3

The creator of this complex arrangement of beams, rods and weights is surely blessed by Ma'at, for it hangs in exact balance. It is all of perfect stiffness, moving as one piece. The beams and rods have been constructed with perfection so as to counter-weight each other around the pivot. Only the values of the weights shown thus needs to be considered. How much does the block bearing the question mark weigh?

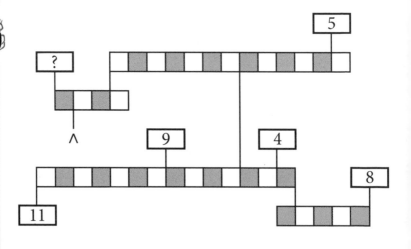

Solution on page 143

GONE GOAT

A farmer is trying to capture a goat that has escaped from its enclosure. The goat has a 10-cubit head start, and in its panic, it is running as hard as it can. It starts out at a speed of 10 cubits a second, but it drops its speed by one at the end of every three seconds. The man sprints after it at his best pace, 6 cubits a second. He stays at that pace throughout, but after 30 seconds he will be forced to stop for a minute or two to get his breath back. Will the man catch the goat?

Solution on page 143

LINE OF SIGHT

An archer is only as good as his line of sight. this map identifies the positions of several individuals, but omits a number of obstructions, each taking up an entire square. The number representing each man tells you precisely how many squares he has in his horizontal and vertical lines of sight, including his own. His sight is blocked by obstructions or by the edge of the field, but not by other archers. No two obstructions touch each other horizontally or vertically. Where are they located?

7			6					7		
			2							
							8			5
	9								7	
							8	11		
4			13		9		5			
				8		5		5		7
		13	17							
	12								5	
4				5						
								5		
			17					11		9

Solution on page 143

RIGHTEOUS PATH

In the ornamental gardens, trees and colonnades combine to shade a certain spiral route from the heat of the noon sun. I have taken the liberty of preparing an illustration of this path. If I reveal that each step of the path is 1m in length, how long is the path?

Solution on page 144

RIDDLE OF THE
SPHINX 3

WHAT IS THE ROOM
THAT, ONCE ENTERED,
CAN NEVER BE LEFT?

Solution on page 144

UNBROKEN

The Mycenean people are capable of a surprising degree of subtlety, if they truly are to thank for this design of distraction. It certainly would go some way to explaining certain of their characteristics. As with other problems of this type, the challenge is to connect the pairs with a single, unbroken line of tiles. The lines move horizontally or vertically, without forming any loops, and without crossing each other. In doing so, they take up the entire grid.

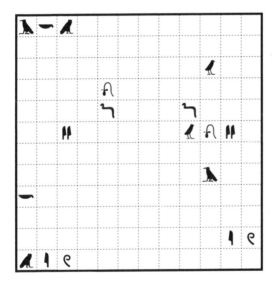

Solution on page 144

·◈· SOLUTIONS ·◈·

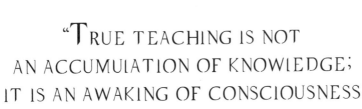

"TRUE TEACHING IS NOT
AN ACCUMULATION OF KNOWLEDGE;
IT IS AN AWAKING OF CONSCIOUSNESS
WHICH GOES THROUGH
SUCESSIVE STAGES"

Ancient Egyptian Proverb

CRATES 1

4	5	2	6	1	3	7
	v		^			
2	4	3	7	5	1	6
3	1	7	5	6	2	4
			v			
6	2 > 1		4	7	5	3
v	^					
5 > 3		6	2	4	7	1
						^
7	6	5	1	3 < 4		2
		v				
1	7	4	3	2	6	5

THREE LOAVES

Each man gets 1/3 + 1/5 + 1/15 of a loaf.

THREE BY THREE

No. Once the players understand how the game works,
it will always end in a draw.

SHADOWS

10.67m.

RIDDLE OF THE SPHINX 1

Man. He in turns crawls as a baby, walks as an adult and uses a walking stick in old age.

UP AND DOWN

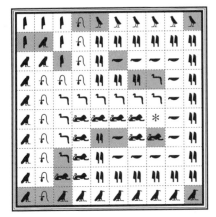

CONNECTIONS

60. Multiply the opposing numbers.

CHARIOTS OF FIRE

The Nile bowmen will make 50 hits, while the chariot
archers will make 48 hits.

DARK SQUARES 1

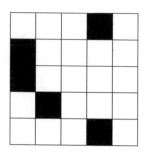

HIEROGLYPHS 1

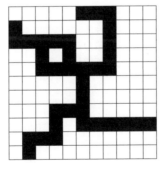

𓅂 = 2

𓅃 = 3

𓄿 = 4

TILES 1

FULL BEAM 1

12.

DOG AND HARE

75 cubits.

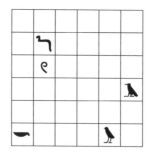

SACRED GRIDS

Each glyph advances 3 squares each time.

TACTICS

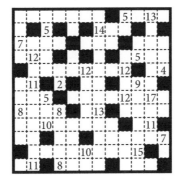

SQUARE OF NUMBERS 1

11	24	7	20	3
4	12	25	8	16
17	5	13	21	9
10	18	1	14	22
23	6	19	2	15

SESHAT'S LOGIC

10:45.

THE ETERNAl

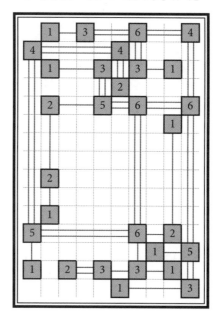

ANCIENT TABlETS

HAE

The three-digit number when added to the numbers on the
top two rows gives the number on the bottom row.
So 4765 = 1017 + 2933 + 815. 8 = H, 1 = A and 5 = E.

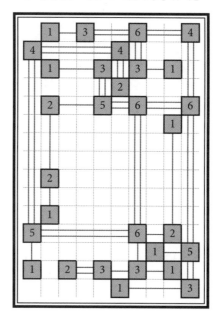

THE MERCHANT

240 khet an hour.

LABYRINTH 1

1	14	■	5	10	■	2	■	12	7
■	4	13	3	■	7	1	5	■	14
2	13	■	10	6	9	■	12	8	4
7	3	14	■	11	8	6	2	9	■
6	■	5	8	12	■	10	■	13	1
■	11	1	■	5	10	■	6	3	■
9	7	■	11	13	■	12	■	5	6
13	■	8	■	9	11	7	14	4	■
■	10	6	2	■	5	■	8	1	12
11	8	■	6	1	3	14	4	■	13
■	12	7	■	3	■	4	■	2	8
12	5	■	4	14	1	8	7	■	9
8	9	4	■	2	■	3	■	14	11
5	■	2	9	7	14	■	10	11	■

A JAR OF ALE

Fill 3, put into 5.
Fill 3 from 8, fill 5.
The 8 now holds two, the 5 holds 5, and the 3 holds 1.
Put 5 into 8, then 3 into 5. Fill 3 from 8, and put it into 5.
8 and 5 now both hold four hinu (~2 litres).

SUN SPOTS 1

0.
Convert the symbols to digits,
and take each row of digits as a number,
and add the numbers.

CHICKENS

9.

LABYRINTH 2

LAST WILL

Rightly or wrongly,
the intent is clear;
if the daughter gets one share,
the mother gets twice that,
and the son gets twice again.
4/7 goes to the son,
2/7 to the mother,
and 1/7 to the daughter.

THE RULE OF ORDER

The sequence is abcdabceabcec, in a horizontal
zig-zag pattern from top left, yielding:

SEMERKHET'S TABLET

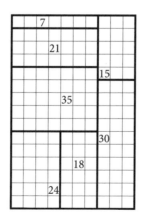

EQUAL SPACE

	7					
		21				
					15	
			35			
					30	
				18		
		24				

POWER OF TEN

340.

———◆———

AHNEN AND BATA

Bata, by 3.

LABYRINTH 3

One route is:

							2			
		6	4	2	0	8	6	4		
		8								
6	4	2	0							
8										
0							8	0	2	
2							6		4	
4	6	8	0	2	4		4		6	8
				6	8	0	2			0
									4	2
				4	2	0	8	6		
			0	8	6					
			2							
		8	6	4						
		0								
		2				8	0	2	4	6
		4				6				8
		6	8	0	2	4				0
							8	6	4	2
							0			

GRAINS OF SAND 1

12.8

CHAINS

21. Each number is equal to the sum of the two before it (starting from 0,1 as givens).

HIGH GRADE GRAIN

20.

SIXES

Six cubes for one six is likeliest — 66% vs 62% vs 60%.

RABBITS

754.

MIGHTY MEHEN

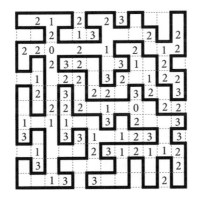

RECONNAISSANCE 1

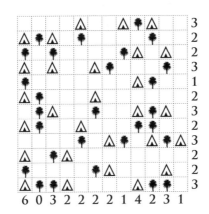

TOKEN GESTURE

𓅃 = 3. 𓅓 = 2. 𓂝 = 6. 𓅱 = 5

CHAMBERS 1

6	6	6	6	1	6	6	6	1	4	4
6	6	1	4	4	1	6	6	6	4	4
9	9	9	4	4	9	9	9	9	9	9
9	9	9	5	5	5	9	9	3	3	1
9	9	9	1	5	5	9	1	3	7	7
1	6	6	6	6	6	1	7	7	7	7
9	9	1	6	1	3	3	1	5	5	7
9	9	6	1	6	6	3	5	5	5	1
9	9	6	6	6	4	4	4	8	8	8
9	9	7	7	7	7	4	2	8	8	8
9	1	7	1	7	7	1	2	1	8	8

DAMNED SOUlS

55. Only the uncertain can (pessimistically) claim damnation, and the virtuous may not claim false uncertainty. 30 + 15 + 10 = 55.

NUMEROlOGY

6+1+4-3 = 8.

YIElD

FUll BEAM 2

10.25.

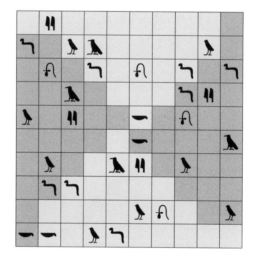

MYSTICAL WISDOM

LINE OF FIRE

			7			6	
11	9				9		
		4		5			
	13	13					
7	9	9					
			8				
		6					
				6		9	9
			6	2			
	7		2				
9				8		7	
13			7				

BEAST FOR SALE

The first man has 16 debens of copper,
the second has 10, and the third has 6.

SHARES

1.5625 hekats of grain. Give yourself a bonus if you thought
to express it with Egyptian fractions, as $1 + \frac{1}{2} + \frac{1}{16}$.

THE SNAIL

It will reach its highest point at
the end of 7 days, 4.43 cubits.
It will not escape.

SEQUENCES 1

Each glyph moves 1 square to the right, then down as many
squares as the number of the column it moved to.

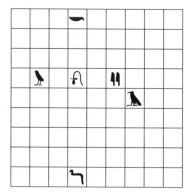

LABYRINTH 4

INHERITANCE

There are just two possible solutions to the
matter. The allocations are either:
2 full, 6 half, and 2 empty; 4 full, 2 half, and 4 empty; and again
4 full, 2 half, and 4 empty, or:
4 full, 2 half, and 4 empty; 3 full, 4 half, and 3 empty;
and again 3 full, 4 half, and 3 empty.

CRATES 2

3 <	5 >	1	6 >	4	2	7
2	7	5	4	3	6	1
1	3	6 >	5	2	7	4
5	6	2	7	1	4	3
7	1	4 >	2	5 >	3	6
6	4	3 >	1	7	5	2
4	2	7	3	6	1	5

NAꝖABA

96.
Each black square is worth the number of its position
on the board (from left to right, with top left being '1').

GRAINS OF SAND 2

Calling a collection of things a 'heap'
is a subjective assessment, so there is no
objective answer to when it loses that quality.

DATES

9

SQUARE OF NUMBERS 2

22	47	16	41	10	35	4
5	23	48	17	42	11	29
30	6	24	49	18	36	12
13	31	7	25	43	19	37
38	14	32	1	26	44	20
21	39	8	33	2	27	45
46	15	40	9	34	3	28

TIME DIAL

8:43:38.

PATH OF AARU

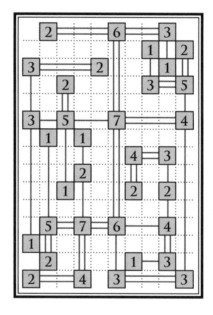

DIGITS

c: F E C. 4939 flipped = 9394.
9394-2741-6000 = 653, F-E-C

BOUNCE

18.

RIDDLE OF THE SPHINX 2

Night and day.

MYCENEAN

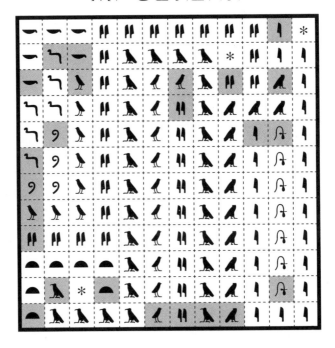

OASES

12. Add or subtract the opposing numbers as required.

DARK SQUARES 2

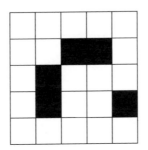

GIYPH

=3. =5. =7. =11.

ROOM SERVICE

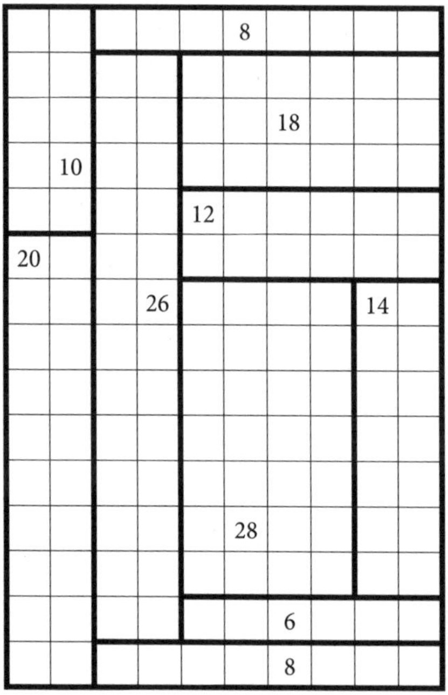

8

18

10

12

20

26

14

28

6

8

BASE TEN

1392.

OUTSIDE THE BOX

Two thirds. You are twice as likely to pull a gold kite from the box with two golds in it, so if you already have one gold, that box will show up twice as often as the box with one gold and one silver.

A WEIGHTY PROBLEM

Just five, weighing 1, 3, 9, 27 and 81 debens. If this seems insufficient, bear in mind that the weights can be added to either or both sides of the balance.

PRIESTS OF RA

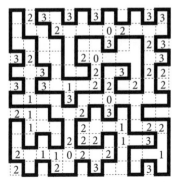

UNLEASHED

The journey takes the man 2.25 hours, so the dog will run 2.25 iteru (a little over 23.5 km).

THE MAZE

One route is:

RIVERS TO CROSS

Let 'A' be a priest and 'a' his novice:

Aa Bb Cc
Bb Cc > Aa
A Bb Cc < a
ABC > abc
Aa B C < bc
Aa > Bb Cc
Aa Bb < Cc
ab > A B Cc
abc < ABC
a > A Bb Cc
ab < ABCc
> Aa Bb Cc

LABYRINTH 5

6		1	8	5		7		11	
9	4	7		3	8	1	14	10	5
1	3	4	2		14		8	9	
3		8		4	7	10	2	5	14
	12		4	8		9		7	
11	5	6	1		2	14	9	13	8
	1	2		13	12		6		4
12	13		6	2		5	7	14	
10	9	12		14	5	2		4	13
	7	13	5		10	12	3		2
5	8		9	12		11		2	6
8		5	10	9	11		4		7
2	6	9		7		4	13	12	11
13		3	7		9	8		1	

FISHLESS

One of the fathers was a grandfather, fishing with his son and grandson. This means that the other father was both a father and a son, and there were only three people fishing.

SUN SPOTS 2

2. Convert the symbols to digits,
and take each row of digits as a number,
and subtract the second row from the top row.

SIMPLE SYMBOLS

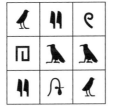

SEQUENCES 2

36. They are those whole numbers which are spelt out
without using the letter 'e', in ascending order.

RECONNAISSANCE 2

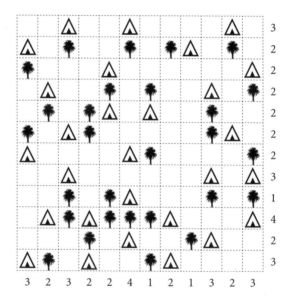

HIEROGLYPHS 2

$\mathbf{A}$ =5. $\mathbf{H}$ =7. $\sim$ =2. $\mathbf{R}$ =1. $\mathbf{J}$ =9

CHAMBERS 2

2	1	9	9	9	9	9	7	7	7	7
2	6	6	9	9	9	9	7	7	7	1
1	6	6	1	6	6	6	1	3	1	4
3	3	6	6	7	7	6	6	3	3	4
3	9	1	7	7	7	1	6	1	4	4
9	9	9	9	9	7	7	1	6	6	6
1	9	9	9	3	1	8	8	6	6	6
3	1	2	3	3	8	1	8	8	1	
3	3	2	4	4	4	8	8	8	1	2
6	6	6	6	4	6	6	6	3	3	2
1	6	1	6	1	6	1	6	6	3	1

SHOTS ON TARGET

Ahmes scored 10. Baenre scored 12. Djedhor scored 9.

FIND THE NUMBER

(20*14) - (12*9) = 172.

BOX OF GEMS

Although the two options look the same, in fact they are completely different situations, and cannot be compared in this way. The issue is an illusion. In either direction, the average worth is 150% of the lower value

TILES 2

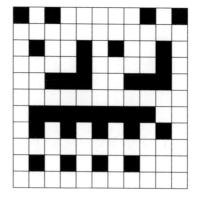

FULL BEAM 3

265.

GONE GOAT

Yes. He will catch the goat on the 30th second, at a total distance of 175 cubits.

LINE OF SIGHT

7			6		■			7	■		
		■	2	■							■
			■			■	8				5
■	9	■		■					■	7	■
							■	8	11		
4		■	13		9		5	■			
				8	■	5	■	5			7
■		13	17							■	
	12			■		■		■		5	■
4	■			5	■						
							■	5			■
		■	17					11			9

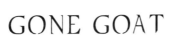

RIGHTEOUS PATH

82m.

RIDDLE OF THE SPHINX 3

A tomb

UNBROKEN

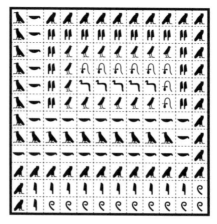